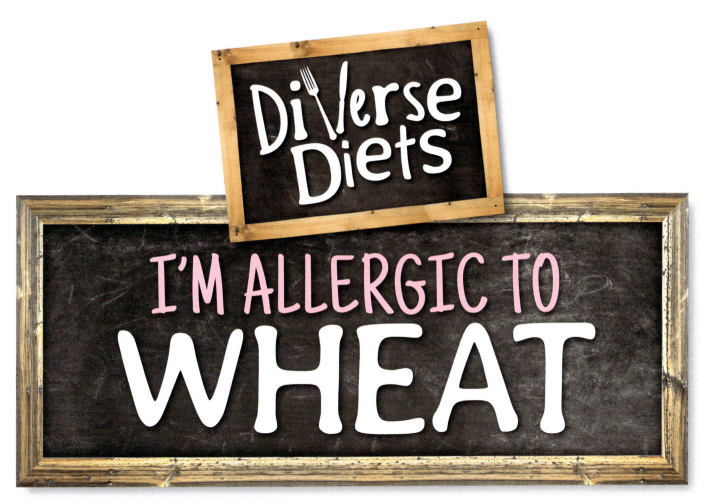

Diverse Diets

I'M ALLERGIC TO WHEAT

By Shalini Vallepur

BookLife
PUBLISHING

©2019
BookLife Publishing Ltd.
King's Lynn
Norfolk PE30 4LS

All rights reserved.
Printed in Malaysia.

A catalogue record for this book is available from the British Library.

ISBN: 978-1-78637-729-6

Written by:
Shalini Vallepur

Edited by:
Madeline Tyler

Designed by:
Dan Scase

Photo Credits

All images are courtesy of Shutterstock.com, unless otherwise specified. With thanks to Getty Images, Thinkstock Photo and iStockphoto. Front Cover – Vitaly Korovin, Irantzu Arbaizagoitia, spb2015, Ku_suriuri, Jane Kelly, Alexander_DG, Galyna Syngaievska. 2 – Irantzu Arbaizagoitia, spb2015, Ku_suriuri. 4 – Rawpixel.com, pikepicture. 5 – pedalist. 6 – Frolova_Elena. 7 – Eakachai Leesin. 8 – kwanchai.c, Sudowoodo. 9 – Teri Virbickis, mcherevan. 10 – Andrii Horulko, Moving Moment, Africa Studio, Steve Paint. 11 – Diana Taliun, P Maxwell Photography. 12 – Maxx-Studio, Tatiana Volgutova, Dinosoft Labs. 13 – Dan76. 14 – alexkatkov, Elena Shashkina. 15 – Phovoir. 16 – Seregam, ifong, sasimoto, Anastasia Petrova. 17 – Mix3r. 18 – In Green, stockcreations. 19 – Michelle Lee Photography. 20 – BravissimoS, Alex Mosiichuk, jujuk suwandono. 21 – Jacek Chabraszewski, uiliaaa. 22 – Alexey Smolyanyy. 23 – Monkey Business Images. Chalk boards – SeDmi. Wood Background – primopiano. Plate – Vitaly Korovin. Notepad – style_TTT.

Contents

Words that look like **this** can be found in the glossary on page 24.

Diverse Diets

There are lots of different foods all around the world. A person's diet is made up of the food that they normally eat every day. Diets can be **diverse**, as different people eat different foods.

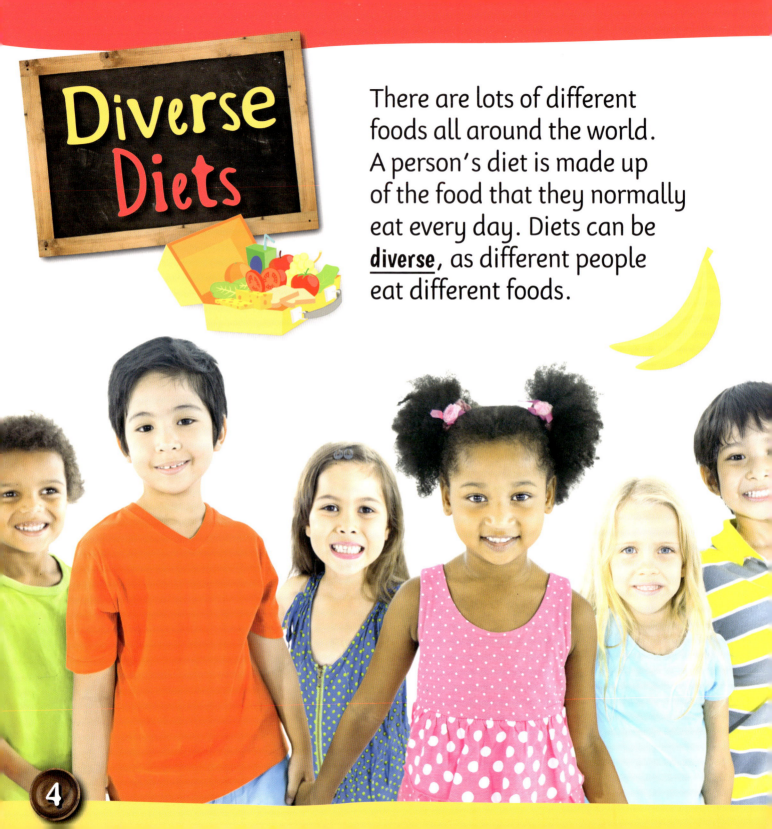

A person might have to change their diet if they have a food **allergy**. They have to make sure that they know what foods they can eat and what foods they can't.

What Is Wheat?

Wheat is a type of grass. We **harvest** wheat and **grind** it to make flour. Flour is used to bake lots of different things.

WHEAT GRAINS

Some people are allergic to wheat. They could get a tummy ache, a rash or be sick when they eat foods that have wheat in them.

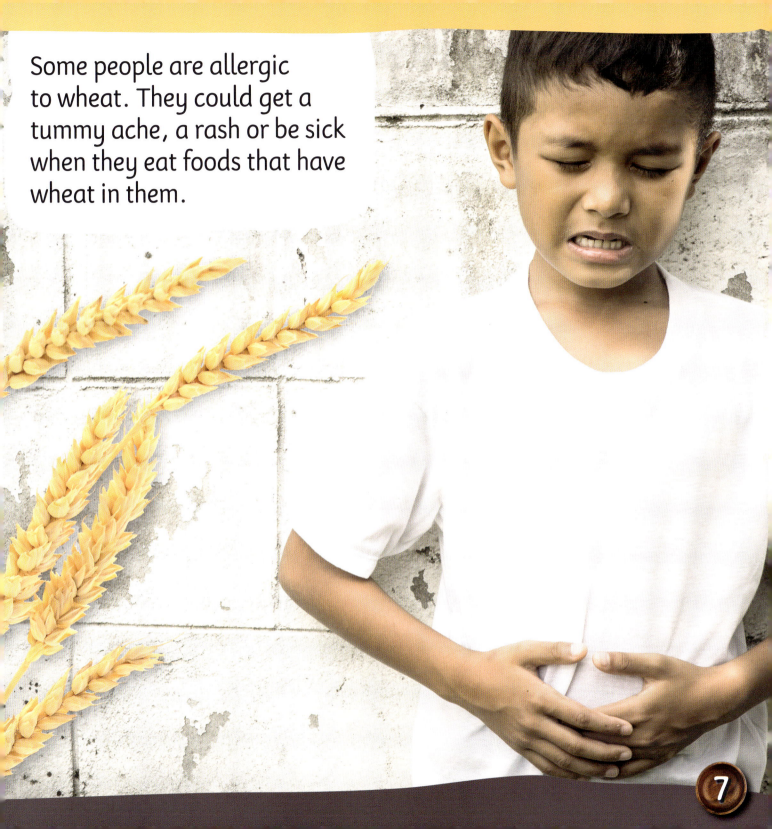

What Does Wheat Make?

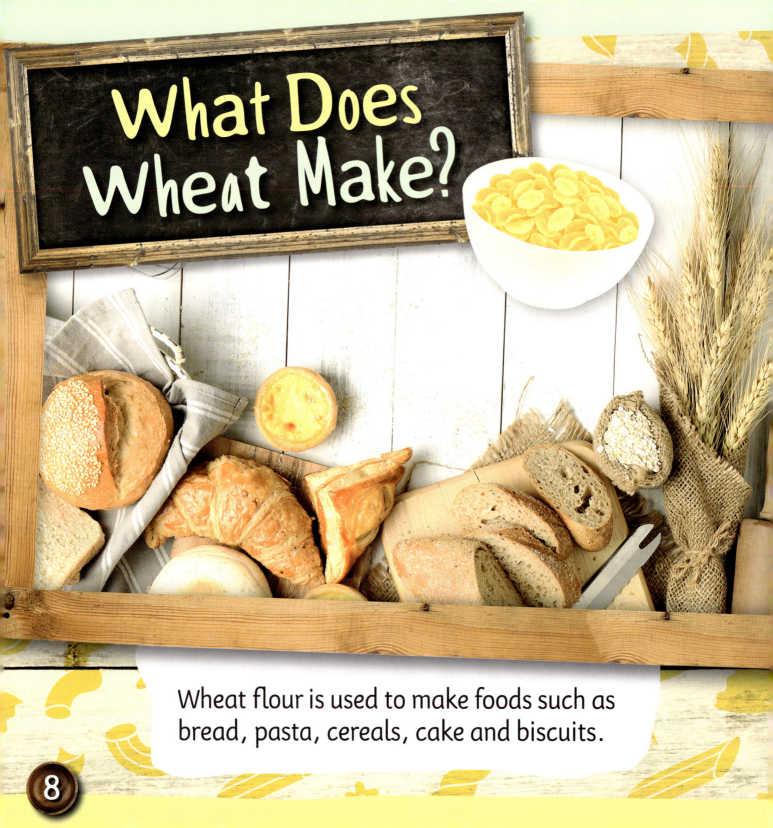

Wheat flour is used to make foods such as bread, pasta, cereals, cake and biscuits.

Wheat has something called gluten inside it.
Gluten makes bread soft and chewy.
Some people get sick if they eat gluten.

GLUTEN-FREE CUPCAKES

Gluten-free foods may still have wheat in them.

Smart Swaps

WHEAT FLOUR

QUINOA FLOUR

BUCKWHEAT FLOUR

MILLET

People with a wheat allergy can buy flour that is not made from wheat. Buckwheat flour, quinoa flour and millet are popular.

Nut flours can also be used instead of wheat flour. Almond meal is made from almonds and ground flaxseed is made from flaxseed.

ALMOND MEAL

GROUND FLAXSEED

Perfect Pancakes

Let's make perfect pancakes using almond meal and ground flaxseed.

A spatula makes flipping pancakes easy.

Equipment you will need:

- Kitchen scales
- Mixing bowl
- Measuring jug
- Measuring spoons
- **Non-stick** frying pan
- Spatula
- Whisk

Ingredients you will need:

- 330 grams of almond meal
- One tablespoon of ground flaxseed
- Half a teaspoon of sea salt
- Half a teaspoon of baking soda
- Three large eggs
- 80 millilitres of **unsweetened** almond milk or milk
- 30 grams of butter

Let's Cook!

1. Put the almond meal, flaxseed, salt and baking soda in a bowl.
2. Crack the eggs onto the flour.
3. Pour in **one-quarter** of the milk and mix everything.
4. Add another quarter of the milk and mix.
5. Add the rest of the milk and mix.

Decorate your pancakes with lots of fruit.

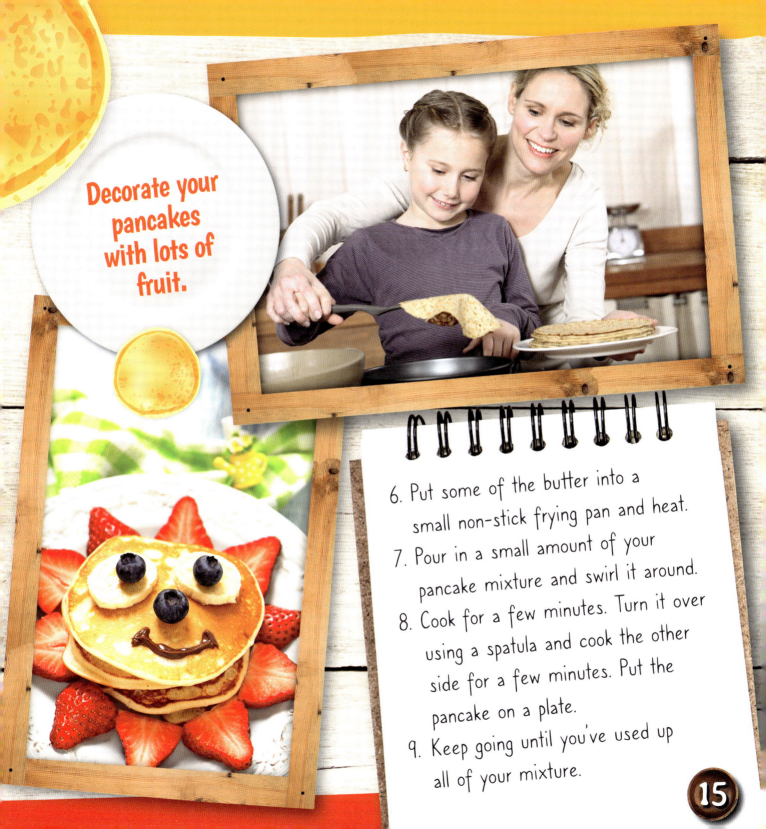

6. Put some of the butter into a small non-stick frying pan and heat.
7. Pour in a small amount of your pancake mixture and swirl it around.
8. Cook for a few minutes. Turn it over using a spatula and cook the other side for a few minutes. Put the pancake on a plate.
9. Keep going until you've used up all of your mixture.

Smart Swaps

BREAD

OATS

OAT CAKES

Some people eat oatcakes and oat crackers instead of bread. They are tasty and can be eaten by people with a wheat allergy.

Some supermarkets sell wheat-free products. Sometimes it can be hard to find the exact food that you need. If you can't find any wheat-free tortillas, you might have to make your own…

Fabulous Wheat-Free Fajitas

Let's make wheat-free tortillas for fajitas.

Equipment you will need:

- Kitchen scales
- Measuring spoons
- Measuring jug
- Mixing bowl
- Baking paper
- Frying pan
- Rolling pin

Ingredients you will need:

- 175 grams of rice flour
- 75 grams of potato starch flour
- 25 grams of tapioca flour
- Two teaspoons of sugar
- One and a half teaspoons of xanthan gum
- One teaspoon of salt
- 250 millilitres of warm water
- One tablespoon of vegetable oil

Xanthan gum helps to make the tortilla chewy like a wheat tortilla.

XANTHAN GUM

1. Put everything in the mixing bowl and **<u>beat</u>** into a smooth dough.

2. Cut the dough into eight pieces that are the same size.

3. Lay the baking paper out and sprinkle some rice flour on it.

4. Use the rolling pin to roll each piece of dough into a thin circle, about 25 centimetres across.

5. Heat a frying pan and put a little vegetable oil on it.

6. Place a tortilla in the pan and cook each side for minute, then remove from the pan.

7. Keep going until all eight are cooked.

Use whatever you like in your fajitas — chicken pieces, chopped peppers, lettuce and salsa will work well.

Living with a Wheat Allergy

For some, wheat allergies can be very dangerous. Anaphylactic shock is a very bad **allergic reaction**. If somebody goes into anaphylactic shock, an auto-injector must be used to help them.

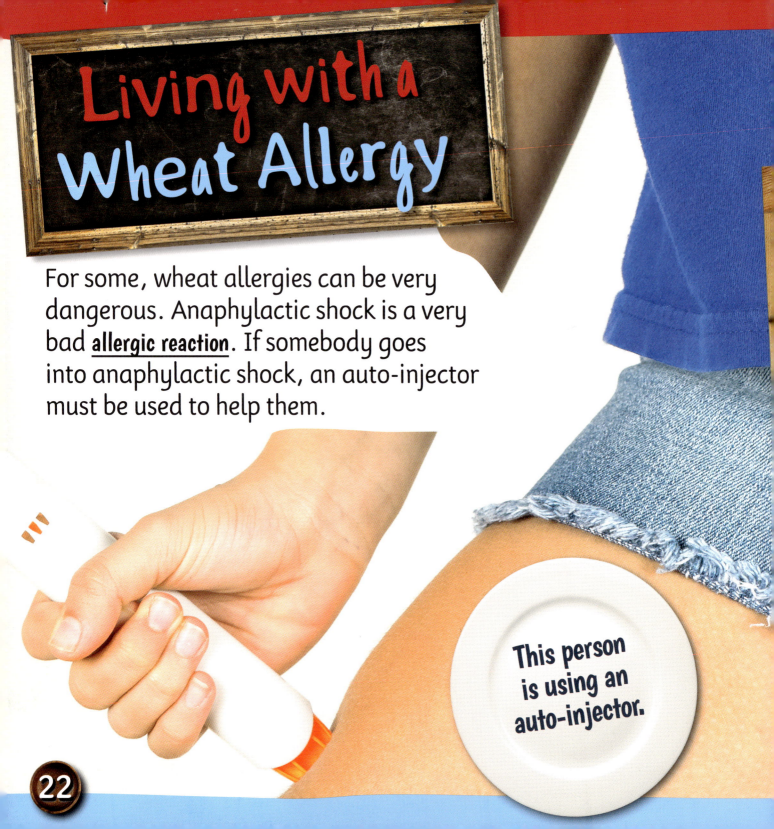

This person is using an auto-injector.

People with a wheat allergy must check food labels and be careful at restaurants to make sure there is no wheat in their food.

Glossary

allergic reaction	getting feelings of illness from something such as nuts
allergy	when the body reacts to something such as nuts, causing feelings of illness
beat	to stir quickly
diverse	different kinds of things
grind	to crush something into very small pieces or powder
harvest	to gather and collect crops
non-stick	when a pan is coated in something that stops food from sticking to it
one-quarter	one of four equal parts of a whole thing
unsweetened	no added sugar

Index